ELIZABETH IN DANGER

S. M. Harrison

Head of Humanities, Knutsford County High School, Cheshire

M
MACMILLAN
EDUCATION

To Anna

First published 1984
Reprinted 1985, 1988

Published by
MACMILLAN EDUCATION LTD
Houndmills, Basingstoke, Hampshire RG21 2XS
and London
Companies and representatives
throughout the world

Printed in Hong Kong

British Library Cataloguing in Publication Data
Harrison, S. M.
Elizabeth in danger.—(History in depth).
1. Great Britain—Politics and government—
1558–1603
I. Title   II. Series
320.942   JN181
ISBN 0–333–35077–4

Cover illustration courtesy of
National Maritime Museum/Photo Michael Holford

CONTENTS

Acknowledgements

The author and publishers wish to acknowledge the following photograph sources:

Reproduced by permission of His Grace The Duke of Norfolk, p. 35 right; by kind permission of The Marquess of Tavestock and the Trustees of the Bedford Estates p. 54 bottom; BBC Hulton Picture Library pp. 12, 18 bottom; British Library pp. 8, 32; Courtauld Institute of Art p. 5; Mansell Collection pp. 6, 10, 24, 33, 35 left, 36, 41, 42 bottom, 44, 49; Mary Evans Picture Library pp. 18 top right, 19 top; National Portrait Gallery pp. 7, 19 bottom, 42 top; National Maritime Museum pp. 40, 43, 46, 47, 48, 53, 55; National Trust p. 16; Public Records Office p. 30; William Salt Library/Peter Rogers Photo p. 28/29.

The publishers have made every effort to trace copyright holders, but if they have inadvertently overlooked any they will be pleased to make the necessary arrangements at the first opportunity.

PREFACE

The study of history is exciting, whether in a good story well told, a mystery solved by the judicious unravelling of clues, or a study of the men, women and children, whose fears and ambitions, successes and tragedies make up the collective memory of mankind.

This series aims to reveal this excitement to pupils through a set of topic books on important historical subjects from the Middle Ages to the present day. Each book contains four main elements: a narrative and descriptive text, lively and relevant illustrations, extracts of contemporary evidence, and questions for further thought and work. Involvement in these elements should provide an adventure which will bring the past to life in the imagination of the pupil.

Each book is also designed to develop the knowledge, skills and concepts so essential to a pupil's growth. It provides a wide, varying introduction to the evidence available on each topic. In handling this evidence, pupils will increase their understanding of basic historical concepts like causation and change, as well as of more advanced ideas like revolution and democracy. In addition, their use of basic study skills will be complemented by more sophisticated historical skills such as the detection of bias and the formulation of opinion.

The intended audience for the series is pupils of eleven to sixteen years: it is expected that the earlier topics will be introduced in the first three years of secondary school, while the nineteenth and twentieth century topics are directed towards first examinations.

1 INTRODUCTION

The threat to Elizabeth

Elizabeth I, Queen of England 1558–1603.
When she smiled it was pure sunshine, but anon came a storm from a sudden gathering of clouds and thunder fell in a wondrous manner on all alike.

Queen Elizabeth I came to the throne at a time of crisis. During the previous thirty years several hundred English men and women had died for their religion. Some of these, like Sir Thomas More, were Catholic. Others, like Thomas Cranmer, were Protestant. Each new reign had brought religious change, and each time a different group was persecuted.

Elizabeth I: the Rainbow Portrait

Left: *The execution of Sir Thomas More, a Catholic who lived in the reign of Henry VIII. He died bravely, with a joke to the executioner and the words, 'I die loyal to God and King, but God first'*

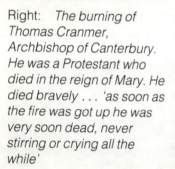

Right: *The burning of Thomas Cranmer, Archbishop of Canterbury. He was a Protestant who died in the reign of Mary. He died bravely . . . 'as soon as the fire was got up he was very soon dead, never stirring or crying all the while'*

Elizabeth wanted to bring this trouble to an end. Her attitude towards religion was that she did not want to 'make windows into men's souls'. She looked for a middle way which would satisfy both Catholics and Protestants. This compromise was the 'Elizabethan Settlement' which established what the national religion would be, and included laws to make sure that everybody worshipped in the same way.

The great majority were content with the settlement, but there were a number of Catholics who were not. Some of these remained in England. Others fled abroad and looked for help to the Catholic countries of Europe, and especially Spain. It is this Catholic threat to the life and throne of Queen Elizabeth which is the subject of this book. We know that Elizabeth survived, but should anyone doubt that the threat to the Queen was real and ever present, they have only to examine the fate of Elizabeth's closest ally.

The murder of a fellow prince

On 10 July 1584 William of Orange, Prince of the Netherlands, was dining with guests. Outside, near the stairs which led up to William's

Philip II, King of Spain. He ruled an Empire which included the Netherlands, part of Italy and South America. He had been married to Mary I, Queen of England 1553–8. He was a strong Catholic, and led the struggle against Protestantism

private chambers, a shabby mean-faced man was waiting. Had anyone asked, he would have told them that he was a messenger known to Prince William. That much was true. What he would not have revealed was that he, Balthasar Gerard, was now waiting for his chance to assassinate the Prince.

William of Orange had been a marked man for some years. He was the heroic leader of the Dutch Protestant states which had joined together to free themselves from the rule of Catholic Spain. King Philip of Spain dispatched an army to restore order in the Netherlands, but he realised that victory would be much swifter if William was disposed of. So in 1580 he issued this order:

> *We do declare him to be a wicked traitor and an enemy to ourselves and to the country. We give permission to all persons ... to arrest, hold and make sure of his person, employing violence if need be.*
>
> *So that our purpose may be achieved more promptly we promise that if there be someone that can rid us of this plague, delivering Orange to us dead or alive, or even just killing him, we will give him the sum of 25 000 gold crowns.*

This order encouraged a number of plots. They included plans to blow up his house, and to poison his dish of eels, but nothing came of them until April 1582. Then, for the first time, an assassin almost succeeded:

> *William was at dinner with a few guests. He led his guests across a big hall to show them a set of tapestries. His bodyguard brought up the rear, but he was not directly protected. Juan Jaureguy pushed through the crowd, carefully levelled the unfamiliar firearm, and released the trigger.*
>
> *Jaureguy gaped, his fingers limp and bloody. Rammed solid with charge and shot, the pistol had blown to pieces, shattering his hand. Swords and halberds flashed into action and the murderer went down under the feet of the guards.*

At first bystanders thought that William was dead. However, an eye-witness was soon to write, 'the ball has done the Prince no other injury than passing through his throat and carrying away two teeth'.

Two years later Balthasar Gerard, a fanatical Catholic, arrived in the Netherlands. Having persuaded the Dutch Protestants that he was on their side, he was entrusted with important messages to take to William. To his surprise, on arriving at William's palace at Delft he was taken straight to the Prince. Gerard was not prepared for such an early opportunity, so he continued to play the part of the honest messenger. William gave Gerard some coins, and it was with this money that Gerard was able to buy two pistols before returning to lie in wait for his prey.

The moment came when William finished his meal and invited his Italian visitor to accompany him upstairs to continue their conversation. William led the way out of the hall, and as he reached the staircase Gerard stepped forward. The ambassador from Venice, who saw the incident, wrote:

> *The Prince of Orange has been shot by a man who pretended that he desired to present a letter to the Prince. The man got quite close to make sure that he would not miss. In the act of handing the letter he put the pistol to the Prince's breast and shot him dead.*

The shot tore through William's lungs and stomach, spattering blood on to the whitewashed wall behind him. He staggered forward crying for pity: 'Mon Dieu, ayez pitié de moi, ayez pitié de mon âme [soul], ayez pitié de ce pauvre peuple'. At this he fell, and soon afterwards died.

The fury of the Netherlanders can be seen in the fate of Gerard:

> *The assassin was captured, put to the torture, and later executed. They tore off his right hand, lacerated his body with red hot pincers, ripped out his heart and flung it in his face. Then they dismembered him and struck off his head.*

The news of William's death was greeted with horror in England. Not only was a heroic ally dead, but furthermore the danger to the life of their own Queen was underlined. Rumour began to circulate that assassins would soon be arriving in England. One letter reached Queen Elizabeth's secretary telling 'of words spoken ... with reference to the murder of the Prince of Orange, that two would come over the sea to do like practice towards her majesty'.

Such threats were nothing new. Various plots against the life of Elizabeth had already been discovered. However, the image of William's broken body, and of the Spanish army pressing forward to overrun the Netherlands, re-emphasised that, truly, Elizabeth was in danger.

Assassination attempt. William Parry, the assassin, failed. Had he succeeded, how would the document in his left hand have helped him?

Questions

1 Look carefully at the portrait of Queen Elizabeth. What can you see on her dress, and what could it mean? Do you think that the portrait might have a purpose?

2 If you are uncertain about the differences between Catholic, Protestant and Elizabeth's 'middle way', look at the table below. Which aspects of the Elizabethan church settlement were borrowed from the Catholic church, and which from the Protestant? Which seems to be halfway between the two? Is there a fair balance?

3 What is there about the life and death of William of Orange which makes it possible to say that Elizabeth faced the same danger?

Elizabeth's middle way

What Catholics believed	Elizabethan Religious Settlement	What Protestants believed
That the church should be ruled by the Pope and bishops.	The Queen would rule as Supreme Governor supported by bishops.	That there should be no Pope or bishops.
That there should be church courts.	Some church courts would remain.	That there should be no church courts.
That Christian belief comes through faith.	There should be limits on what preachers could say.	That Christian belief comes through preaching the Bible.
That the most important ceremony is the mass.	There should be no mass.	That there should be no mass.
That services and the Prayer Book should be in Latin.	Services and the Prayer Book would be in English.	That services and the Prayer Book should be in the native language.
That saints should receive special prayers.	Saints should receive no special prayers.	That saints were unimportant.
That churches should be highly decorated and services full of ceremony.	Churches should be decorated and some ceremonies should be allowed.	That churches and services should be plain.
Priests should wear bright robes.	Bright robes should be allowed.	That plain robes should be worn by churchmen.

RECUSANTS, PRIESTS AND PUNISHMENTS

Recusants

The Tichborne family of Hampshire were people who refused to accept Elizabeth's church. The lives and deaths of two of them show what could happen to Catholics in England. Nicholas Tichborne was loyal to his Queen, but refused to worship in anything but the Catholic way. For this he was fined until, as he wrote:

> *he had one little farm to support his wife and children upon and it had been seized by royal officers ... and he himself made a prisoner.*

He wrote begging for his liberty so that he could try to borrow enough to pay the sheriff, and to support his wife and eight children. However, in 1589, after nine years in prison, he died. He was penniless, and did not even have a Christian burial.

His nephew, Chideock Tichborne, was a Catholic who not only refused to conform, but also plotted against Elizabeth. He was discovered and suffered a traitor's death:

> *He was only twenty-eight when he died, his handsome head almost pulled off his neck by the extra long rope on the high gallows, and his body disembowelled while he was still alive, in front of crowds so densely packed that they were sprayed with his blood.*

Pope Pius V 1566–72. He was a sincere man, deeply concerned about the religious conflict of his time. However, he did not understand politics, and his followers thought his order against Elizabeth was a mistake

excommunication: a person who is excommunicated is cut off from the Church and from God. This was a terrifying sentence to a Catholic, but did not worry Elizabeth as she no longer acknowledged the power of the Pope

Chideock and Nicholas Tichborne and their families, and many other families like them, were known as recusants. Recusants were Catholics who would rather suffer punishment than attend the new church services. A few of them, like Chideock, plotted against the Queen. Most, like Nicholas, remained loyal. But they were regarded as a danger to Elizabeth because their loyalty was divided. As English citizens it was their duty to obey the Queen in all things. However as Catholics it was their duty to obey the Pope. When in 1570 the pope ordered Catholics to do all they could to overthrow Elizabeth, the recusants had to choose between the two.

The Pope's order said this about Elizabeth:

> *that she had seized on the Kingdom and monstrously usurped the place of Supreme Head of the Church.*

As a result he declared:

> *Elizabeth as being an heretic to have incurred the sentence of excommunication ... and we do command and charge all noblemen, subjects, people ... not to obey her orders.*

Elizabethan government:
at the head was the *Queen*,
who was very powerful. She
had one or two *Principal
Secretaries* who were close
advisers. Most of the work of
government was done by
the *Privy Council*, rather like
the Cabinet today.
Parliament was needed to
raise taxes and pass laws,
but usually did as it was told
by the Queen and Privy
Council. *Justices of the
Peace* made sure that laws
were enforced locally

There were important mistakes in the papal order, which enabled Catholics to ignore it without betraying their beliefs. However, because a few took the order seriously, all recusants were regarded as a threat.

The government therefore took action against them. At the start of the reign anyone who did not attend church services was fined one shilling for each time he was absent. This was a light punishment, and often the fines were not collected – especially in the north of England where the Catholic religion was stronger and the Justices of the Peace often sympathised with the recusants. However, as time passed, punishments became more severe, as shown in this timeline:

1570–71 The Queen's Privy Council, fearing that recusants were escaping punishment, asked for lists naming them to be properly completed and for fines to be collected.

1580 Fines were increased to twenty pounds per month. Those who could not pay would lose their land.

1585 Instead of paying fines recusants could provide for a horseman in the Queen's army and from 1586, recusants were imprisoned in specially appointed castles such as Wisbech, Hatton and Framlingham.

Exercise

In each case there is a reason for the change of policy. Divide your page in two. In the left-hand column briefly state the date and policy. In the right-hand column say why the policy was changed. You will find the reasons for this on pages 14, 26 and 28.

In the light of what you have read here, and the answer to the last question, summarise why the government thought that recusants were dangerous.

Life became hard for many recusants. As well as having to pay heavy fines many, like Nicholas Tichborne, lost their land. Furthermore recusants were not allowed to hold government posts and were treated with deep suspicion by old friends, neighbours, and sometimes even by their own families. As the Spanish ambassador reported in 1564, 'the evil lies in universal distrust, for a father dares not trust his own son'.

Despite these hardships recusants continued in their faith, and the fines paid to the government each year totalled £6 000. No doubt the Queen and her ministers had hoped that the heavy fines would force the Catholics to conform. The fact that they did not was blamed on the influence of the missionary priests who were coming secretly into the country, especially after 1580. The government now turned its attention to them.

The missionary priests

From 1568 onwards young English Catholics were trained to become missionary priests at Douai in the Netherlands. From 1580 onwards others were trained as members of the Jesuit order of priests in Rome.

These priests came with two main purposes: to keep the Catholic religion alive in England, and if need be, to die for their faith. From the Catholic viewpoint those who died were martyrs. On the other hand the government could only view them as traitors. They were, after all, a threat to Queen and country at a time when Catholics abroad, led by Spain, were trying to launch an invasion of England.

Dangerous priests. This picture shows two priests. What is one of them holding in his right hand? What did the government fear that this would cause them to do? What warning is given to priests in this picture?

Martyrs or traitors? Historians still argue this point today. So, too, do they argue about the work of government in searching out the recusants. For example, two completely different opinions lie behind these two statements about the work of the Queen's Principal Secretary Sir Francis Walsingham, in the campaign against missionary priests:

Sir Francis Walsingham: he became a Principal Secretary in 1573. He was a strong Protestant, serious, determined and loyal. He worked to root out all of Elizabeth's enemies

Walsingham shows in his behaviour unmistakeable marks of brutality and fanaticism. Blinded by religious passion he believed every Catholic priest was dangerous to the state and he conducted their examination in person.

Alternatively:

Walsingham was, on the whole, opposed to the execution of priests 'saving a few for example's sake'. Taken as a whole his policy was a policy of mercy. The result of his advice eased considerably the fate of the missionary priest.

Exercise
Which key words in the quotations show how the writers' opinions differ about Walsingham's treatment of priests? Why do you think that recent historians still disagree so much about these issues?

The job of the historian should be the search for truth about the past. Often this will involve the ability to see and understand both sides in a dispute. This chapter will now look at the lives and deaths of missionary priests from two viewpoints. First it will consider the priests' own view, then it will show how the government dealt with the problem which the priests posed.

Missionary priests – preparation

Some hundreds of young men aged between fourteen and twenty-five left England and Wales to train at Douai or Rome. The main aim of their training was to put aside all personal comforts and ambitions. Instead they were to become dedicated to serve God and to give up their whole life to Him. Most important of all was:

martyr: this is a term for people who have suffered death for their religion, whatever that religion might be

the contemplation of suffering and death of the martyrs which lay before them in fulfilment of their desire to die for England's conversion.

Here are some of the rules which students had to follow:
  i)   The day would begin with meditation and prayer at 5 a.m. Prayers would then be said regularly throughout the day.
 ii)   Meals would be taken in silence, except for Bible readings.
iii)   Students must exercise in the art of debate. They must not be sarcastic, irritable or hot-tempered.
 iv)   They must not go out alone, or correspond without permission.
  v)   Students must be clean, tidy and punctual at all times.
 vi)   Students breaking minor rules would not receive full rations and be made to look ridiculous by eating from a plate on the floor.
vii)   A student breaking an important rule would be dressed in a large garment like a sack with holes for the eyes and a large hole in the back. He would then whip himself until the blood flowed.

Exercise
Which of these rules was designed for:
a)   Preparation for preaching?
b)   To make individuals seem unimportant?
c)   To prepare for torture and death?

It is important to note that the missionary priests were told to discuss only religion, and not to make any attack in word or deed on the Queen or government. The most famous missionary priest, Edmund Campion, said, 'I never had mind and am strictly forbidden, to deal in any respect with matters of state or policy of the realm'.

The government's view – traitorous priests

The government feared that the priests were a grave danger to Elizabeth, and that they were not solely concerned with religion. They believed this because:

1 Priests came secretly from Catholic countries abroad, including Italy, France and Spain.
2 They had been trained in colleges which received support from England's enemies, including the Pope and Philip of Spain.
3 Once in England the priests were said to 'run from county to county and house to house and do draw by persuasion numbers of her Majesty's subjects'.
4 As supporters of the Pope, the priests were bound to follow his orders. At worst this would include the assassination of Elizabeth, for it was said that 'whosoever sends her out of this world with the pious intention of doing God's service not only does not sin but gains merit'.

Exercise
a) Rephrase the quotations from 3 and 4 in your own words.
b) Only one of these fears concerns religion alone. Which one?
c) What other fears were present which led the government to regard priests as traitors?

The priests' view – the secret ways

Once trained, the priests made their way to England. Fourteen of them arrived in 1580 alone. Some went by secret ways and others travelled by normal routes.

One of the most famous of the priests, Father Gerard, chose the secret ways:

After making careful choice of place for landing they secretly landed at night and, carefully avoiding all human habitation and every barking dog, they spent the first night in the woods despite the rain and cold.

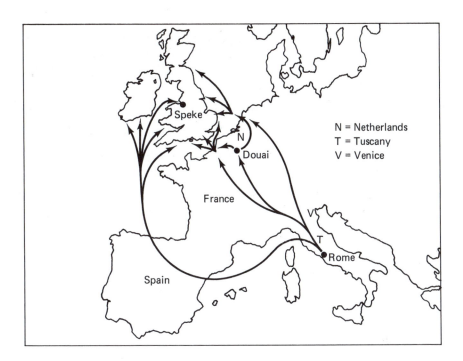

N = Netherlands
T = Tuscany
V = Venice

Robert Parsons, on the other hand, set out from Calais 'disguised as a soldier with buff and gold and a soldierly swaggering manner'. Edmund Campion himself travelled as a merchant trading in precious stones. Other disguises included that of a doctor and a gentleman in silk velvet carrying a falcon.

Once in England the priests made their way to the houses of Catholics whom they knew to be in sympathy with their cause. Usually these Catholics were wealthy recusants who were able to pass off the visitors as friends or servants, or hide them in some secret corner of the house. Penalties for hiding priests were harsh, so recusants took great care that they were not discovered. The most dangerous time was when services were held, as can be seen from this description of a service held by Edmund Campion:

Word would go round that Campion had arrived and throughout the evening Catholics of every degree, squire and labourer, would stealthily assemble. Before dawn a room would be prepared for mass. Watches were set in case of alarm. Then Campion would preach to a hushed audience, every member of whom was risking liberty and fortune, and perhaps his life, by attendance. A few words of leave taking, then the horses' hooves clattered once more in the cobbled yard. Campion was on his way again.

Within the large houses of wealthy recusants it was possible to build 'priest hides'. Some of these were primitive home-made affairs but some recusants employed experts such as Nicholas Owen to construct hides in their houses. Owen had his own special way of building a hide:

Whenever possible he made a hide within a hide with an escape route if the hide was discovered. He also tried to arrange some system by which those inside could communicate with friends in the house and receive provisions if the search went on for long.

Ingenious hides exist all over the country. At Towneley Hall, Burnley, entry to the priest hide:

was gained by lifting the tread of a small stairway which gave access to a spacious room, the floor of which consisted of a mixture of clay and rushes. This floor, some twelve inches thick, set hard and completely deadened all sound.

In the same house a priest could pass from the chapel through a 1.8 metre wall to a secret stairway. From there he could escape to the outside or to the other parts of the house via the upper gallery. In the chapel itself concealed behind ornate woodwork above a doorway, was a place where the sacred vessels used in Catholic services could be hidden before the priest escaped.

An ingenious hide. What would have made this hide particularly difficult to find? Is there anything wrong with it?

The hide at Speke Hall: The priest would open a panel to the left of the chimney, climb up a rope ladder, pull it up, put down a trapdoor, and then edge his way along to a spacious hiding hole that would be heated by the chimney! There were two alternative escapes from the hide. This picture shows the hide as it can be seen today

Speke Hall

Father Gerard tells of another hiding place reached by 'raising part of the floor under the grate of a fireplace on which wood was kept'. Using such places of hiding Gerard was able to survive in England for nearly twenty years. Often he was in great danger. He recalled how once he was 'concealed in a cupboard behind the wainscot (panelling) of a room for a few days.... At the end of the time he was released from the hiding hole half dead'.

Gerard was an exception. Few priests survived so long. Some were caught on entering the country and most did not last a year before being caught.

Exercise
Look at the map showing routes from the colleges into England, and some of their possible destinations. Which routes might be the safest? Why? How would you have reached Speke Hall from Rome?
  Try to find some examples of priest hides in your area.

The government's view – *searching for priests*

At the time when the problem of priests was at its height the task of catching them fell to Sir Francis Walsingham. He had several different sources of information. First he was informed by ambassadors and continental spies that priests were on their way to England. Secondly a watch was kept at the ports. Walsingham:

> had searchers stationed at all the places where priests were wont to land, and these searchers not only scrutinized all travellers coming from foreign parts but also very often stopped the posts carrying letters and examined their packets.

Thirdly Walsingham had six double-agents working as searchers in England. Usually these men pretended to be Catholics. One way in which they won the confidence of Catholics was by being imprisoned amongst them. One agent, Robert Barnard, boasted to Walsingham of his success:

> I was never in better credit with the Papists ... for I have attained the means to have access to all the prisons in London ... whereby there is nothing that shall come over or go over, nor anything be done here within our country but I am assured to hear thereof.

Another spy, Maliverney Catlyn, first appeared in Portsmouth Jail. He was transferred to Marshalsea Jail in London and it was there that he heard information concerning Spain's preparation for the invasion of England. Walsingham's most successful spy was Richard Berden.

He moved freely among Catholics in London and infiltrated a group which had been set up to help Jesuits. He worked efficiently as their representative in London for two years, and was not discovered. His success in deceiving the Jesuits is shown by the words of Robert Parsons, who wrote of Berden twenty years later 'he did well'.

Walsingham also received information from people who were not spies on his payroll, but who hoped for reward for information received. This meant that any casual observer at a church service or in the house of a recusant could turn into a government informer.

The most controversial source of information was the dreadful torture chamber. Once a priest had been captured he was tortured to see if he had any more knowledge which might be useful to the government.

A prisoner, Edward Rishton, gave this account of the torture chamber:

Of the means or instruments of torture employed in the Tower there are seven different kinds. The first is the Pit, a subterraneous cave twenty

Pair of thumbscrews

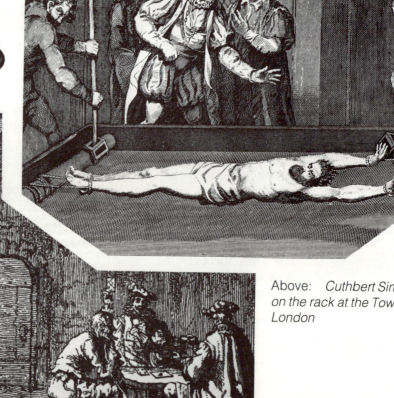

Above: *Cuthbert Simpson on the rack at the Tower of London*

Left: *Man being tortured 1592*

'Scavenger's daughter'

feet deep and entirely without light. The second is a cell or dungeon so small as to be incapable of admitting a person in erect posture: from its effect on its inmates it has received the name 'little ease'.

The third is the rack, on which by means of wooden rollers and other machinery, the limbs of the sufferer are drawn in opposite directions.

The fourth is called the 'scavenger's daughter'. It consists of an iron ring which brings the head, feet and hands together until they form a circle.

The fifth is the iron gauntlet, which encloses the hand with the most excruciating pain.

The sixth consists of chains or manacles attached to the arms, and the seventh of fetters by which the feet are confined

These cruel instruments were carefully designed to inflict pain rather than death – to get the victim to tell all he knew before his body was broken. Torture was used mainly from the 1580s when fear of Catholics was at its height and it was justified by saying that any information given would make the Queen and her country safer.

Exercise

Using the outline plan given, complete the diagram to show the sources of information received by Walsingham. Some have already been completed to help you.

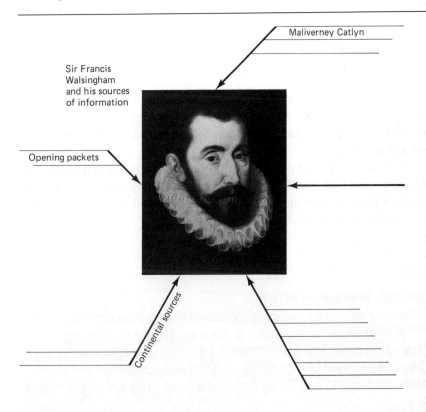

Maliverney Catlyn

Sir Francis Walsingham and his sources of information

Opening packets

Continental sources

Once information was received about the location of priests a search was made. Sometimes the priests were forewarned and had already escaped. At other times the searchers could not find the priests they were so well concealed in ingenious hides.

Often, though, the priests were caught. Edmund Campion's whereabouts were discovered by luck, but the way in which he was searched out shows the thoroughness of the government officers involved.

A searcher named Eliot arrived at the house of well-known recusants at Lyford in Berkshire. He hoped to surprise some priests but could not have dreamed that anyone as famous as Campion would be there. The house surrounds a courtyard, and was fortified with gate tower, moat and drawbridge. Eliot gained admission by asking for the cook by name. Naturally, convinced that Eliot was a fellow Catholic, the cook asked him if he would like to join the mass. Eliot went up and joined three priests, three nuns and twenty-seven others. After the ceremony Eliot excused himself and rushed for help. Shortly afterwards, he returned and the house was surrounded. By the time that he was allowed back inside, the altar, beads and books were hidden away, Campion and the two priests were hidden behind some panels in a secret room, and the other visitors who had not left before Eliot's return were concealed in the dovecote.

The first casual search revealed nothing. The magistrate was satisfied but Eliot demanded a more thorough search. They discovered the men in the dovecote, which prompted them to search further:

Methodically, room by room they went through the house, sounding the panelling and splintering it where it seemed hollow; they found several secret places, but no sign of priests.

Nothing further had been found by dusk, and so a guard of sixty men surrounded the house to prevent anyone leaving. At daybreak the search began again. Eliot began to wonder whether Campion might not already be gone.

Just as he was giving up hope a chink of light was spotted in the well over the stairs. The wall was broken open to reveal the three priests. Their discoverer, Jenkins, called out 'I have found the traitors'. They were taken to London to face the final test.

Exercise: Find the priest hides

Follow the directions to locate the priest hides at Speke Hall.

The searchers have made a scale plan of the house using measuring rods. The plan shows the outside walls and corridor. They suspect one or more hides, and intend to make internal measurements to see if they can find a hide. They know that in this

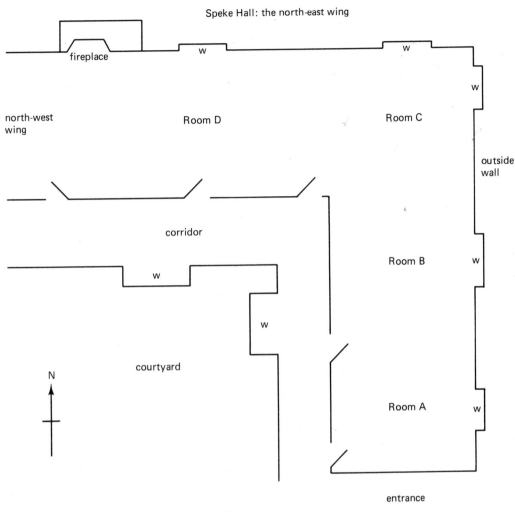

Speke Hall: the north-east wing

fireplace

w   w

w

north-west
wing

Room D

Room C

outside
wall

corridor

Room B   w

w

w

courtyard

N

Room A   w

entrance

wing there are four rooms, one with a fireplace. The scale is 1 mm
to 1 foot. Trace, or very carefully draw the given outline. In turn
measure the size of the rooms. Draw the dividing walls on the plan,
allowing one foot for the thickness of each wall.

Room A is 27 feet long from the south wall.

Room B is 38 feet long from the south wall.

The searchers know that the south wall of room C is a
continuation of the west-east corridor wall. Draw it in, and include a
fireplace ten feet wide and three feet deep on the western end of
the wall.

Room C is 65 feet long from the east wall.

Room D is 31 feet long from the east wall.

Have you discovered any areas which are unaccounted for or
which do not appear to have a purpose? You should have found
two!

Describe the search for priests, telling the story *either* from the
viewpoint of the hunter *or* the hunted. The class should hear
examples from both sides.

The priests' view – the death of a martyr

Waiting in his cell the priest knew that the true test of his faith had come. He would have to face a barrage of questions, torture, and a terrible death. But even while he lay thinking of these things he was 'forced to lie, continually booted and clothed many weeks together, pined in his diet [starved], consumed with vermin and almost stifled with stench'.

Yet in one sense this was what all their training had been for. They believed that martyrs could do more than anything else to save the Catholic religion in England. As Campion said:

be it known to you that we have made a league . . . cheerfully to carry the cross you shall lay upon us and never to despair of your recovery, while we have a man left to enjoy your Tyburn or to be racked with your torments or consumed with your prisons.

Bravely Campion faced torture, not confessing even when 'iron spikes were driven between the nails and the quick until the nails of his fingers and toes were turned back'.

Father John Gerard was taken to a deep underground chamber where there was an upright pillar with iron staples at the top. His wrists were put into iron gauntlets and fixed at each end of an iron bar which passed through the staples so that he was left hanging. Asked if he would confess:

'I cannot and will not,' I answered. But I could hardly utter the words, such a gripping pain came over me. It was worst in my chest and belly, my hands and arms, and I thought that blood was oozing from the ends of my fingers and the pores of my skin. The pain was so intense that I thought I could not possibly endure it.

The Lord saw my weakness . . . He sent me relief . . . He gave me the most merciful thought: the utmost and worst they can do is to kill you, and you have often wanted to give your life for your Lord God . . . From that moment the conflict in my soul ceased, and even the physical pain seemed much more bearable than before.

With similar thoughts to these, other priests were able to face death with great courage. Campion, charged with treason, declared his innocence to the last. Standing on the gallows at Tyburn he prayed:

'For Elizabeth, your Queen and my Queen unto whom I wish a long quiet reign with all prosperity'. The cart was then driven from under him, the eager crowd swayed forward, and Campion was left hanging until, unconscious, perhaps already dead, he was cut down and the butcher began his work.

Campion had fulfilled his mission and the Catholic church had gained another martyr. Campion was one of 130 priests executed.

Tyburn: Tyburn was the usual place of execution, and stood in London where Marble Arch stands today. The public attended executions, but seem to have shown more pity, than bloodlust for some of the brave victims

The government's view – death to traitors

The government thought of these priests not as martyrs to be respected but as traitors to be despised. To make it quite clear that their purpose was not just to preach religion, but to overthrow the Queen, all priests were asked 'the bloody question':

> If the Pope in his bull pronounces her majesty to be no lawful Queen ... and if the Pope or any other by his authority do invade the realm, which part [side] would you take, or which part ought a good subject of England to take.

Campion refused to answer, and so he was declared a traitor. At his execution this was made clear to the audience when a government minister called out 'this was not a case of religion but of treason'.

By saying that priests were traitors the government was doing its best to avoid making Catholic martyrs. Of course, no martyrs need have been made at all if the priests had been imprisoned and not executed. Why, then, were so many sentenced to death?

The answer lies in the challenge to Elizabeth provided by Mary, Queen of Scots, and the growing probability of war with Spain. Elizabeth and her ministers were frightened of the influence of these priests and the way in which they might be able to rally Catholics to help Mary or the Spaniards. As one modern historian has written:

> The plans of Philip II against England which resulted in the dispatch of the Spanish Armada aroused the English Council to take measures which in ordinary times they would not have taken. The persecution of priests should be regarded essentially as a war measure.

Exercise

The last two sections of this chapter have been about the motives of priests who suffered torture and death, and the motives of the government officers who punished them.

With a partner, or as a group, prepare an interview between yourself and *either* a priest or a torturer/executioner. Think carefully about what questions you would be likely to ask, and what answers you would be likely to receive. Write this up as a dialogue, some of which may be read to the class.

Topics of conversation might include:

For the priest: reasons for coming to England, capture, feelings about torture and execution, summary of achievement.

For the torturer: why torture, techniques used, feelings about the victims.

---

3 | MARY, QUEEN OF SCOTS

The threat

Mary, Queen of Scots

On a spring day in 1568 a small fishing boat arrived at Workington on the Cumbrian coast. Observers would have seen a tall woman stepping ashore, but few would have recognised her. Disguised in borrowed clothes and with her red hair cropped close, she was Mary Stuart, Queen of Scots. This striking woman had come to England in disgrace having escaped from imprisonment by her own subjects. The charge against her was that she had a part in the murder of her second husband, Lord Darnley. His strangled body had been found in the wreckage of his house, which had then been blown up to conceal the crime. Worse still, the reckless Mary had then married the Earl of Bothwell, the man suspected of the murder. Now she had come to England, protesting her innocence, to ask Elizabeth for help in regaining her throne.

Elizabeth was most unhappy to hear of Mary's arrival. Her presence in England created grave problems. The greatest of these was that Mary had a strong claim to succeed Elizabeth on the English throne. Further, Mary was a Catholic. We have seen that there were still Catholics in England, some of whom would join in an attempt to overthrow Elizabeth. Catholic countries abroad, especially France and Spain, might be willing to supply an army to invade on Mary's behalf.

Elizabeth was forced to make a swift decision. She refused to see Mary until she had been cleared of suspicion of having a part in Darnley's murder. Neither would she release her to seek refuge in France or Spain, where she could cause more trouble. Instead she decided to keep her as an honoured prisoner, and she began talks with the Scots to try to restore Mary to her throne.

Mary, Queen of Scots
1542 Born, and became Queen six days later.
1558 Married to King of France, who died in 1560.
1561 Returned to Scotland, now a Protestant country.
1565 Married Lord Darnley, who later murdered her secretary.
1566 James Stuart was born, later James VI of Scotland, James I of England.
1567 Darnley was murdered.
       Mary abdicated in favour of James and was imprisoned.
1568 She escaped and fled to England.

Mary showed little gratitude. Within a few weeks of her arrival in England she asked the servant of the Spanish ambassador to pass on this message:

if his master [the King of Spain] will help me I shall be Queen of England in three months and Mass shall be said all over the country.

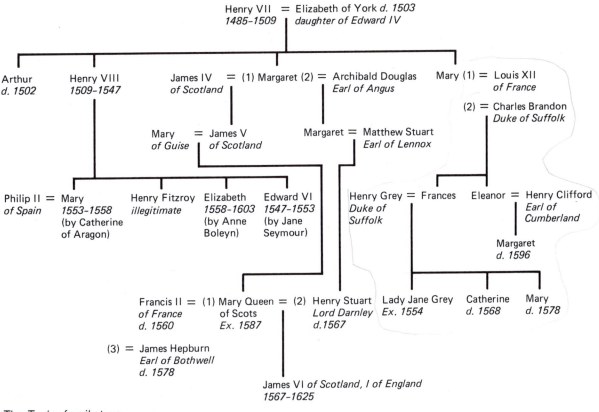

The Tudor family tree

Exercise
Look carefully at the Tudor family tree. Was there anyone alive in 1568 with a better claim to follow Elizabeth on the throne than Mary?
The text above describes Mary as reckless. Is there any accompanying evidence to support such a judgement?

Rebellion and plots

Elizabeth's worst fears about Mary soon proved to be real. In 1569 a rebellion broke out in the north of England. It was led by the Earls of Northumberland and Westmorland, who had been plotting to marry Mary to the Protestant Duke of Norfolk. Then they intended that

Duke of Norfolk: Thomas Howard, Duke of Norfolk, was England's foremost noble. He was a Protestant, but came from a Catholic family. He was greatly respected, and Catholics thought that England might accept Mary as Queen more readily if she was married to him

Elizabeth should name Mary and Norfolk as her successors so that the Catholic religion would eventually be restored. However, the rising collapsed and the rebels were defeated. Many executions followed and the laws against Catholics were tightened up, but Mary and Norfolk were spared.

Only two years later they were the subject of another plot. On this occasion an Italian named Roberto Ridolfi claimed to have 6 000 Spaniards waiting to join the English Catholics in an attempt to replace Elizabeth with Mary and Norfolk. This plot was also poorly planned, and it is not difficult to find why it failed:

Ridolfi was a crack-brained schemer, ready with childish irresponsibility to put the name of any nobleman or man of worth into a list of potential rebels and, with simple faith, construct a vast rebellion on paper.

Also:

Elizabeth received a private warning from the Grand Duke of Tuscany who had learned all too easily of Ridolfi's hazardous plans.

Exercise

Which phrase in the first extract suggests that the Ridolfi plot was never a serious threat?

Look at the map of Europe on page 15. Where is Tuscany? What does that suggest about European knowledge of Ridolfi's plans?

The English people, and especially the Members of Parliament, were furious when they heard about this new threat to the life of the Queen. They had demanded Norfolk's head after the Northern Rising of 1569. Now their demands were much louder. Norfolk had promised to be loyal, and now that his promises had been broken the Queen sadly was forced to agree to his execution.

Mary was spared, but in 1583 yet another plot was discovered. An Englishman named Francis Throckmorton was found to have taken part in a plot to launch the 'Enterprise of England'. This was the plan for a full-scale invasion of England by Catholic countries backed by the Pope. Its purpose was to overthrow Elizabeth and put Mary on the throne.

The plot was discovered by Sir Francis Walsingham's network of spies:

In May 1582 a messenger was intercepted near the border. The man was disguised as a dentist and among the paraphernalia of his trade he carried a looking glass at the back of which important letters were concealed.

Throckmorton was arrested and tortured:

> *though at first he withstood the rigours of examination and even the torment of the rack, his courage at last gave way. 'Now,' he moaned, 'I have disclosed the secrets of her who was the dearest thing to me in the world ... faith broken, honour lost.'*

Demands for the death of Mary now reached fever pitch. Consider this advice about the fate of Mary, given by Parliament, (A and B) and Sir Francis Walsingham (C):

A   *May it therefore be enacted [made law] that if Mary shall make any claim or stir any war or rebellion that said Mary shall be deemed and taken a traitor and being thereof convicted shall suffer pains of death.*

B   *In the event of any attempt being made on Elizabeth's life with a view to advancing some person to the throne, not only to disallow that person's succession but to kill him – or should we say her, by any means they could.*

C   *Set her head upon a spike on London Bridge where it could contrive no more plots and might nod a solemn warning to all intending traitors.*

Now consider why Elizabeth rejected this advice, as explained by Elizabeth herself (D) and two modern historians (E and F):

D   *What [will] my enemies say when it be spread that for the safety of herself a maiden Queen could be content to spill the blood, even of her own kinswoman.*

E   *That closeness which two Queens and near cousins should feel for each other, so often chanted by Mary, may have more echoes in Elizabeth's heart than she ever admitted.*

F   *Elizabeth could not bring herself to execute a divinely ordained sovereign [that is, a monarch appointed by God].*

Exercise: Should Mary be executed?

Look at documents **A**, **B** and **C**. These documents all urge Elizabeth to kill Mary, but disagree about the circumstances under which she should be killed. Match up each document with one of the three following statements.

a)   Kill Mary if anyone plots against Elizabeth on her behalf.
b)   Kill Mary.
c)   Kill Mary if she plots against Elizabeth.

Using documents **D**, **E** and **F** give three reasons why Elizabeth would not execute Mary.

Which do you consider to be the best advice from **A**, **B** or **C** and which the strongest reason for ignoring it from **D**, **E** or **F**? Justify your answer.

Francis Walsingham has been described as 'Mary's declared enemy first to last'. He wanted to end the danger posed by Mary once and for all. However, he realised that Elizabeth would not consent to execution until she was convinced by positive proof that Mary was actually involved in a plot against her life. Walsingham very cleverly obtained this proof by skilfully weaving together two different plots. He was then able to present the evidence to Elizabeth so that she would have to agree to Mary's execution.

The secret post

During the years of Mary's captivity she was moved from place to place and the net of security around her was steadily tightened.

In January 1585 she was moved to Tutbury in Staffordshire. Whereas Mary had previously been kept in comfort, she must have been horrified to see her new prison. Tutbury was a large grim castle. Not only was it partly ruined, damp and draughty, but it overlooked a reeking marsh which made the castle a most unhealthy place.

As well as having to suffer these dreadful conditions, Mary was allowed no visitors, and her servants were allowed no contact with castle servants. When she did leave Tutbury for any purpose her guards were instructed not to 'pass through any town nor suffer the people to be in the way where she shall pass'. The only person she was allowed to write to was the French ambassador, but she knew that all such letters were opened and read by Walsingham. We can be sure that all of these rules were enforced, because her jailer was Sir Amias Paulet, a stern puritan who had no sympathy for the Queen of Scots.

Mary desperately wanted to write in secret to her supporters in England and abroad. Walsingham wanted to be sure he knew of any secret post system which Mary was using. He therefore decided to set up a post himself and trick Mary and her supporters into using it.

This could only be done by using a double agent; someone working for Walsingham but trusted by Mary and the Catholics. This man was the unprincipled Gilbert Gifford. Catholics trusted him because he was the cousin of a leading English Catholic who was exiled in France. Gifford came under Walsingham's control when he was arrested while trying to get into England. Rather than face punishment he agreed to work as a double agent.

Mary became ill at Tutbury, and was moved to a warmer and more pleasant manor house called Chartley in Staffordshire. It was more comfortable there, but security was just as tight. Imagine Mary's delight when she first received a secret letter. It was brought into Chartley by a local brewer who made regular deliveries at the house.

Gifford had paid the brewer to hide letters in his beer kegs. The letters were wrapped in waterproof leather packets and were small enough to go through the bung holes of the kegs. (Neither Gifford nor

Tutbury Castle. Do you think it would have been a good prison?

28

the brewer realised that the other was also being paid by Walsingham!) On the return journey the brewer passed letters from Mary to Gifford. He returned secretly to Chartley and gave them to Sir Amias Paulet. Paulet then passed them on to an agent named Phelippes who was Walsingham's expert forger and decoder.

Phelippes' decoding skills were not required as one of Mary's first letters had given the key to the cipher which would be used in all her later messages. Phelippes simply applied the code, copied out the message and sent it on to Walsingham. The original was very carefully resealed and returned to Gifford, who then delivered it to the French Embassy and collected letters to be taken back to Mary. These simply followed the same route in reverse. So it was that all Mary's secrets were being read by Walsingham, yet Mary suspected nothing.

Exercise: The secret code
Complete this diagram. In the top section of the box write the name of each person in the secret post, and below state what happened to the letters while in their care.

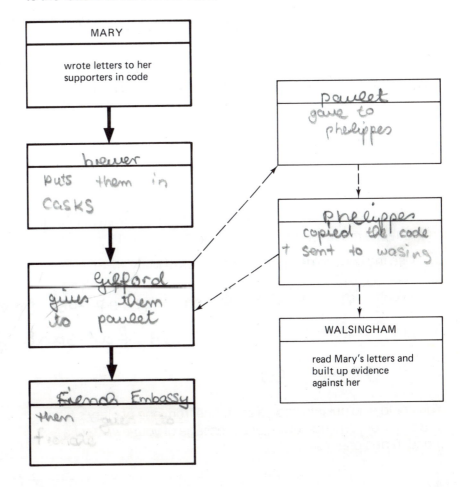

MARY
wrote letters to her supporters in code

brewer
puts them in casks

Gifford
gives them to paulet

French Embassy
then gives to fisher

paulet
gave to phelippes

Phelippes
copied the code + sent to wasing

WALSINGHAM
read Mary's letters and built up evidence against her

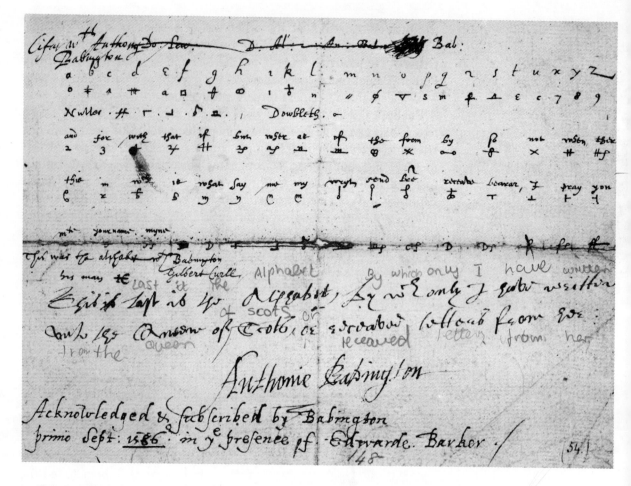

This is Mary's secret code, and a confession relating to it signed by Anthony Babington, one of Mary's supporters (see page 31).

a) Use the sentence above Babington's signature to help you place these words in the correct order:

only letters written Scots Alphabet w^ch (which) from or unto Queene receaved her last is the the This have of by.

b) Use the code to decipher these words of Mary's:

You could also put into code a sentence from one of Mary's letters to Babington, printed above, or a message of your own. Get a friend to decipher it.

The Babington Plot

While Walsingham was setting up the secret post for Mary, another plot was forming. Some 'young hare-brained Catholic enthusiasts' living in London were putting together a most dangerous plan to overthrow Elizabeth and put Mary on the throne. Their leader, Anthony Babington, was described as a young man of 'enchanting manner and wit ... quick intelligence and considerable daring'. However, he lacked one essential quality: caution. Amongst the errors which he made was to set all his plans down on paper. He also arranged for a portrait of the conspirators to be painted before the plot was nearly ready! Furthermore he believed greatly exaggerated stories about an invasion force gathering on the continent which would back up his efforts.

Walsingham knew of Babington's intrigue before he had created the secret post to Mary – the information came from a double agent named Poley who had been planted in Babington's group. It only remained for Walsingham to allow Mary contact with these plotters so that he could obtain the proof of her treason.

By coincidence there was, amongst some other confiscated letters in his possession, a letter to Mary from her friends in Paris which mentioned Babington. The letter suggested that Mary should contact him as he might be of some use to her. Walsingham now passed this letter of introduction into the secret post, and sat back to await results.

Mary quickly responded to the letter by writing to Babington. He must have been overwhelmed by her encouraging letter, because he responded, giving full details of the plot. These details included the preparation of an invasion force, the securing of ports where it could be landed, and the rescue of Mary and a hundred of her followers. Most important of all, the letter mentioned six 'noble gentlemen' whose task would be 'the dispatch of the usurping competitor' – in other words, the murder of Elizabeth.

Mary warmly welcomed the plan and offered detailed advice about her own rescue. She suggested three alternatives:

a) That she might be rescued while out walking as her guard was quite small.
b) That 'at midnight ... set fire in the barns and stables and whilst my guardian and his servants run forth to the fire your companions might surprise the house'.
c) That her rescuers might hide in delivery carts and that 'just in the middle of the great gate the carts might fall down and you might come suddenly with your followers and carry me away'.

Later in the letter Walsingham was given his proof. Mary made reference to the assassins saying that once 'the forces be in readiness without and within, then it shall be time to set the six gentlemen to work'.

Babington and the plotters

The letter was copied by Phelippes, and in an attempt to obtain more information he forged a postscript:

> *I would be glad to know the names and qualities of the six gentlemen . . . for it may be that I shall be able, upon knowledge of the parties to give you some further advice.*

The whole letter was then resealed and passed on to Babington. He did not respond immediately, and rather than take any further risks Walsingham invited him to his house and trapped him there. Babington managed to escape to St John's Wood, but finally he was driven out by hunger, captured and taken to the Tower of London. There he confessed and gave details of the whole plot, little knowing that Walsingham knew all his plans already.

Finally on 20 September 1586 Babington and six others were taken to the gallows on St Giles Fields. There they suffered all the horrors of a traitor's death: 'drawing to the place of execution upon an hardle or sled where they be hanged until they be half dead, and then taken down and quartered alive; after that their members and bowels are cut from their bodies and thrown into a fire provided near hand'.

Exercise

There are clues here that Babington and Mary were poor plotters. Make a list of all the evidence you can find to support such a view.

Look carefully at the engraving on the next page. It shows a famous execution after Elizabeth's death. Are all the stages of execution described above, pictured here?

Hanging, drawing and quartering

Trial and execution

Walsingham now turned his attention to Mary. She was arrested while out hunting and her rooms were searched. Elizabeth's ministers now demanded a trial on a charge of treason. The Queen was unhappy but agreed.

The trial began at the castle of Fotheringay in Northamptonshire. Mary not only denied the charges against her, but would not even admit that the court had a right to try her. To this day historians argue her guilt or innocence.

Either on your own or as a class consider these points of evidence.

GUILTY	NOT GUILTY
Mary had plotted rebellion since arriving in England	Mary was a prisoner in England for sixteen years and was justified in trying to escape
Mary had written letters to enemy powers abroad	Mary could not obtain a fair trial in England
Mary was a Catholic queen who threatened the English Church	Evidence against Mary was extracted under torture
Mary was a criminal who murdered her husband and deserved to pay for it	The Babington Plot was arranged by Walsingham
Mary had repaid Elizabeth's protection with ingratitude	The letters to Babington were forged
Mary had written to Babington agreeing to the plot to kill Elizabeth	Mary was a queen appointed by God who could not be tried in England

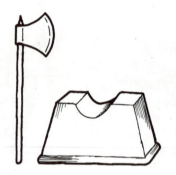

Six are given for each side. You may like to discuss any other arguments that you have seen in this chapter, but make sure that you keep an equal number on each side. Then consider the strength of each argument and give it a mark out of ten. Your class may wish to argue about the strength of each point in turn. At the finish your totals will show your verdict.

On 13 October 1586 Mary was found guilty, and ministers demanded her death. Elizabeth reluctantly signed the death warrant, but still would not issue it. She suggested to Paulet that he should poison Mary. Paulet, a deeply religious man, responded saying, 'God forbid that I should make so foul a shipwreck of my conscience'.

Finally Elizabeth agreed, and nearly four months after being found guilty, Mary was informed that she was to be executed on the next day, 8 February 1587. On her last evening she ate little, gave some of her possessions away to servants and friends and wrote some letters. She did not undress or sleep, and her maidservant read to her. At dawn she prayed, said farewell to her servants, and was led to the great hall at Fotheringay where the execution was to take place:

A sketch showing the scene at Mary's execution. She is seen twice here. What does a comparison between the sketch and a) the description of the execution; and b) the evidence provided by the prayer book and rosary, which survive today, tell us about the accuracy of the sketch?

Her progress being ended, the executioners, kneeling, desired her Grace to forgive them her death: who answered, 'I forgive you with all my heart, for now, I hope, you shall make an end of all my troubles'. Then they, with two women helping her up, began to disrobe her . . . and all this time she never changed her countenance but with smiling cheer uttered these words 'that she never had such grooms to make her unready and that she never put off her clothes before such a company'. . . . she kneeling down upon the cushion . . . without any fear of death she spake aloud this psalm in latin . . . Then groping for the block, she laid down her head, putting her chin over the block . . . Then she, lying very still upon the block, one of the executioners holding her slightly with one of his hands, she endured two strokes of the other executioner with an axe, she making very little noise or none at all: and so the executioner cut off her head, sawing one little gristle, which being cut asunder he lift up her head to the view of all the assembly and bade God save the Queen.

So ended Mary, Queen of Scots. In London the news of her death was greeted with joy. Elizabeth, however, seemed furious. She said that the execution had been a mistake, and that she had not intended the warrant of execution to be sent. Possibly this was true, but possibly she was unwilling to accept the responsibility for the death of her cousin.

Mary, Queen of Scots was dead, but the Catholic threat was now even greater. Philip of Spain had never been enthusiastic about invading England on Mary's behalf. But in her will Mary gave Philip her title to the English throne. This gave him an extra reason to move forward with his plans for the invasion of England.

Exercise

This chapter contains evidence about Mary's later life. Using what you have read here and a reference book for other facts, write an obituary. You may be sympathetic towards Mary or critical of her – an obituary is a place where judgements can be made.

THE SPANISH ARMADA

The Spanish Armada, the greatest challenge to Elizabeth, was first sighted in the Channel on 19 July 1588:

The Spanish fleet was stretched out in the form of a half moon with an immense distance between its extremities. The masts and rigging, the towering sterns and prows which in height and number were so great caused horror mixed with wonder. It came on with a steady and deliberate movement, yet when it drew near in full sail it seemed almost that the waves groaned under its weight and the winds were made to obey it.

At last, after growing hostility between England and Spain, King Philip II had decided to invade. Partly he wanted to lead a crusade to return England to the Catholic faith. Partly it was the result of his anger against Elizabeth and English interference in Spanish affairs. Elizabeth had been helping Protestant rebels in the Spanish Netherlands to rise against their Spanish overlords. Also English sailors led by Drake and Hawkins had been raiding Spanish colonies in Central America and attacking Spanish treasure ships.

Netherlands: the Netherlands had been giving its Spanish rulers trouble since 1563. An army was sent to stop rioting, but in 1574 rebellion broke out and the Protestant Dutch provinces broke away from the Spanish Empire. Elizabeth helped the rebels in their fight against Spain, which the Dutch were to win in 1609

The mighty Armada pursued by the English ships

Exercise: The decision to launch the Armada

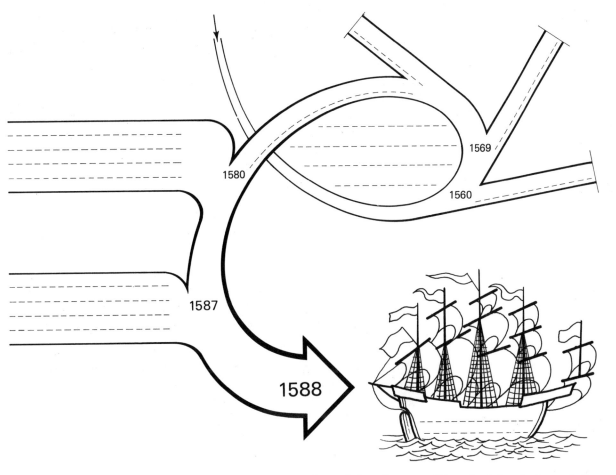

Draw your own version of the diagram 'The decision to launch the Armada'. Then write the following details in the correct place, using the words underlined.

a) The arrow represents Philip's desire for a Catholic England.

b) The alternative schemes to make England Catholic which failed included marriage to Elizabeth, rebellion by Catholic subjects, and assassination of the Queen. Two additional factors urged Philip on.

c) The first was English action against Spain. Elizabeth helped the rebels in the Spanish Netherlands, her sailors made attacks on the Spanish Empire, and Spanish treasure ships were captured.

d) The second was the execution of Mary, who made Philip her heir to the throne. According to Catholics Elizabeth was illegitimate, so Philip could now claim the throne.

e) The outcome was the decision to launch the Armada.

The invasion plan

Philip had begun his plans for an invasion long before he actually decided to send the Armada, and by 1585 war seemed inevitable. At first he hoped for a direct invasion from Spain, but he was advised that he would need over 550 ships and nearly 100 000 men. This would have been far too expensive. Then he thought of a new idea: he already had an experienced army waiting in the Netherlands. It only required a fleet strong enough to defeat the English navy, and with the Channel under Spanish control the army of the Netherlands could be ferried across to begin the invasion. Philip hoped that English Catholics would support his army in an attack on London.

Here are some comments made about this plan:

1   *The King never saw his Armada. He did not always understand what he was doing. Especially he didn't understand seafaring or navigation.*

2   *He did not realise the difficulty of getting a sail-driven sea-borne force to turn up at the right time and place. To sail over hundreds of miles of water dominated by a determined enemy, to sweep that enemy aside and still be at the rendezvous on time. It was in fact impossible.*

3   *Perhaps no monarch about to launch a war was so mistaken about his enemies. Philip was led to believe that the Protestants of England were a small minority: that the majority were Catholics who would gladly rise in revolt when they sighted the Armada.*

Exercise

The Pope was asked by Philip to contribute one million ducats to help pay for the Armada. You are the Pope's advisor. Would you recommend that: —

a)   He should give him the money.
b)   The money should only be given on certain conditions.
c)   He should refuse to provide any money.

Justify your answer.

Philip did not think that details of the plan were important. He would have agreed with his ambassador Mendoza who said that it was 'God's obvious design to bestow upon your Majesty the crown of the two kingdoms'. What does this statement show about the reason for Spanish confidence in the success of the Armada?

The two fleets

Finally Philip's plan was put into action and the Armada sailed for England. There, English sailors were preparing to defend their Queen and country in what promised to be one of the greatest sea battles of all time. This chapter will analyse the strengths of each side in turn. The exercise on page 43 will ask for a direct comparison to be made. In command was the Duke of Medina Sidonia. He had only been appointed a few months before, and on hearing the news had written unhappily to Philip:

I wish I possessed the talents and strength necessary for it. But Sir, I have not the health for the sea. I soon become seasick. It would not be right for a person like myself, possessing no experience of seafaring or war, to take charge of it.

Despite his protests he found himself in the flagship *San Martin* with the tremendous task before him. He was no great leader but he was a very brave man who, more than anything else, wished to carry out his mission with honour.

His officers were also poorly chosen for command of the fleet. They were aristocratic, proud, and superbly brave, but they were soldiers and not sailors.

Most of the other men who sailed with the Armada were soldiers too. Apart from 180 priests on board the fleet, there were 27 000 soldiers and 8 000 sailors. The reason for having so many is explained by a modern historian:

In a Spanish galleas the soldiers regarded themselves as the most important people. They avoided fighting at sea if they could, but if they had to their only method was to tell the sailors to lay the ship alongside the enemies, and then to board it and fight hand to hand with the weapons used on shore:

However, there were sufficient sailors to handle the fleet, there being one man to every two tons of shipping. These were regular seaman with experience in the Atlantic or the Mediterranean, and they could rely on the soldiers to man the guns during battle.

The Ships

The Spanish ships were built to give the soldiers on board as much help as possible:

The galleons were 64 in number, being of a huge size and very stately built and so high that they resembled great castles. The lower works and timbers were out of measure strong, being framed of planks and ribs four or five feet thick.

A galleas

Escorial: this was Philip's palace in an isolated part of central Spain. He spent years planning and building the palace with a monastery, school, library and hospital. Thereafter he shut himself away and was seen less and less. It was from here that he planned the Enterprise of England *galleys, galleons and galleases:* galleys were the traditional fighting ships of the Mediterranean since ancient times. They were driven by hundred of slaves rowing with great oars. They rammed enemy ships, holing them below the waterline. Galleons were great sailing ships which fought with cannon and by boarding. Galleases were half way between the two, powered by oar and sail. It was hoped that they would combine the best features of each – in fact they combined the worst

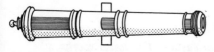

One type of cannon used at the time of the Armada

These were the newest galleons in the Spanish fleet, and most of them had been converted from older ships during the last two years. The reason for this sudden modernisation was that the old fleet had been smashed by Sir Francis Drake at Cadiz in April 1587. Drake, having heard of the preparation of a great fleet, had sailed into the Spanish port of Cadiz and found, as he recalled:

sundry great ships, some laden, some half laden, some ready to be laden with the King's provisions for England. We stayed there and sank one vessel of 1 200 tons, burnt a ship of 1 500 tons and 31 ships more. We carried away four with us laden with provisions.

The Spanish ships at Cadiz had been outsailed and outgunned. Even in the Escorial, his remote palace, Philip had realised the significance of this raid. Many of the ships were out of date and useless in this kind of warfare. The galleys in particular were obsolete, and suitable only in the tideless Mediterranean Sea. Whereas Philip had intended to send forty galleys, only four galleases finally sailed. In their place he used the royal galleons normally reserved for guarding his convoys to America, and he quickly converted forty large merchant vessels to make them into warships. This conversion was done by adding great castles fore and aft. He now had 64 galleons, 4 galleases, 32 lighter fighting ships, and 25 storeships.

The guns

Drake's raid on Cadiz had also shown the weakness of Spanish gunnery, and much had been done since to improve it. This table shows the total firepower of the Armada:

Type	Number	Weight of shot in lb	Range in paces
Cannon	163	50	1 700–2 000
Perrier	326	24	1 600
Culverin	165	17	2 500
Demi-Culverin	137	9	2 500
Saker	144	5	1 700
Minion	189	4	1 600

This improvement gave the Spanish far more heavy cannon than the English. On average, Spanish ships had a broadside twice as heavy as the English ships.

Conditions at sea

The English may have hoped to be able to avoid these heavy broadsides by attacking the weaker vessels first, but Spanish tactics made this impossible. The whole Armada adopted the crescent formation with the strongest ships around the outside and on the wings. In this formation the fleet was ordered to make its way to Calais without diversion.

Soon after it had left port the poor sailing qualities of the Spanish ships became obvious. The high castles made the galleons hard to handle, and they travelled only five miles in the first three days. Storms blew up and the fleet was scattered until eventually shelter was found in Corunna. During this time conditions must have been terrible for the soldiers. They were kept below deck where the air was poor, there was no sanitation, and seasickness affected the strongest stomachs. It must have been like living in a cesspit.

Worse still the food was rotting and the water was green with slime. This was because much of the food and water had been barrelled a long time before the Armada sailed. The inevitable result of such conditions was diarrhoea and disease. Corunna gave the fleet a chance to gain fresh stores, but even so by the time the Armada reached England it was reported that rations were reduced to 'just enough to keep them alive, namely half a pound of biscuit, a pint of water, and half a pint of wine daily, without anything else'.

Fortunately for the Armada, a fair wind took it swiftly from Corunna to England. The Spanish sighted Lizard Point in Cornwall on 19 July 1588. A map of the route of the Armada can be seen on page 52.

The defence of England

While the Spanish preparations were nearing completion, Elizabeth still hoped for peace. Negotiations were taking place with Philip's commander in the Netherlands, the Duke of Parma. As long as there was a chance that war might be avoided Elizabeth was unwilling to spend money on defence.

England had no standing army, but in case of invasion men were being trained to defend the coastal counties. The most likely places for an enemy attack, such as Plymouth, had the largest forces, but even there only 2 000 men were prepared. However a system of beacons was made ready to relay the news of an invasion to London so that the government was warned and reinforcements could speedily be brought into action.

England was difficult to defend. There were many possible landing places, and the Queen's forces were thinly spread and not easily moved. Therefore hopes rested on the first line of defence, the English fleet.

The English fleet

The men
The western fleet was waiting at Plymouth under the command of Lord Howard of Effingham. Elizabeth had chosen well. Lord Howard was a cabinet minister, a noble, and a charming and tactful man who

the Tudor army: all men between sixteen and sixty had to attend musters once yearly. They were registered, trained and had their equipment checked. When required, commissioners took the men they needed from the musters. The system was corrupt and inefficient, but the English army was better equipped and fed than most

Howard of Effingham

Portrait of Sir Francis Drake. Why do you think symbols such as the globe, helmet and coat of arms appear in the picture?

The Ark Royal. *Howard's flagship, built in the new style*

could handle fiery characters like Drake and Frobisher. Sir Francis Drake is the man most associated with the Elizabethan navy. There is a legend that Drake was playing bowls when news came that the Armada had been sighted. According to the story Drake calmly announced that he would finish his game first, then deal with the Armada. Whether this is true or not, it seems to be typical of the cool courageous character of the man.

For some years Drake had waged a personal war against the Spanish with the secret approval of Elizabeth. He was the first Englishman to sail round the world. He took tremendous risks, as in the attack on Cadiz, but his crews had great respect for him and would follow him anywhere. Furthermore Drake was a Protestant with a particular wish to gain revenge on Catholic Spain, and he was the Armada's greatest enemy. The Spanish called him El Draque, the Dragon.

Below Howard, Drake and the other famous captains such as Hawkins, Frobisher, Raleigh and Grenville were a force of men in which sailors outnumbered soldiers by 14 300 to 1 500, an average of one sailor to every two tonnes of shipping. Recently wages had been raised from 6s 8d to ten shillings a month to attract more able sailors. They were mainly experienced seamen used to the rough conditions of the Atlantic and to sea warfare.

The ships

Their ships, too, were far better for these waters than the Spanish galleons. They were about the same length, but the ships of the latest design were built without castles. In other words they were 'razed' of their castles, and because of this they were known as race-built ships.

San Juan de Ulua: in 1567 a fleet led by Hawkins and including Drake was forced by a hurricane into the port of San Juan de Ulua in Central America. Despite a safe conduct Hawkins was treacherously attacked by a Spanish fleet, losing three-quarters of his ships

John Hawkins: Hawkins was the son of a Bristol merchant. In early slave trading voyages he came into conflict with Spanish ships. After the incident at San Juan de Ulua he became treasurer of the navy. He was responsible for the new breed of English warships

The Golden Lion, *an older English ship. What differences are there between this and the* Ark Royal?

They appeared to be smaller than the galleons because they lay closer to the water. This made them much more seaworthy and they could make circles around the ungainly Spanish ships. There were twelve of these in the western fleet, plus fifty older first line ships and forty-three smaller ones.

The guns
Their guns were also different.

Type	Cannon	Perrier	Culverin	Demi-Culverin	Saker	Minion
Number	55	43	153	344	662	715

On balance the English had more long-range guns but carried a lighter broadside than the Spaniards. The purpose of the English ships was not to come to close quarters but to sweep past, firing a broadside.

Stores
If the English ships and guns were superior, their supplies were certainly not. The story of the provisioning of the English fleet was a disaster from first to last. Whereas the Spanish were provided with supplies (albeit rotten ones) for six months, the English were supplied only on a day-to-day basis. Howard complained constantly of the need for more supplies, but a letter allowing the fleet to take up stores for twenty days did not arrive until they had sailed. Therefore the English crews, too, were on short rations, and the only item available in plenty was badly brewed beer.

Exercise
Divide your page into two, or use a double page. Using the information above make a table which compares the two fleets. Use the following headings and provide enough detail to make comparison possible: Leadership: Seamen: Soldiers: Ships: Guns: Stores: Tactics.

Stalemate

The first meeting of the two fleets set the pattern for what was to follow. The Spaniards, seeing the English fleet coming out of Plymouth, anchored. This would have left the English fleet to the east, giving the Spaniards the advantage of being on the windward side. But, to Medina Sidonia's amazement, by the following morning the English had come round to the west. This manoeuvre would not have been possible for the clumsy Spanish fleet which could not sail to windward.

The Armada off Dodman Point. The diagram shows what happened off Plymouth. Using the text, explain the diagram

Then, with constant skirmishing between smaller groups of English vessels and the Spanish crescent, the fleets made their way up the Channel. Like terriers the English snapped at the edges of the crescent. Occasionally when the wind dropped, the galleases took their chance to counter-attack. Worried that the Armada might enter the Solent, Drake's squadron cut off the entrance. But Medina Sidonia had his orders to sail to Calais without deviation. He closed up the Spanish formation by threatening to hang the captain of any ship that left its station. The only damage done was to one Spanish ship which was sabotaged, and to two which collided. One of these, the *Rosario*, fell behind and was captured by Drake.

Finally after nine days the Armada crossed to the French side of the Channel and anchored at Calais. The first stage of the battle was over.

Exercise

Look back at your table comparing the two fleets. Why was it always likely that the fleets would reach Calais undamaged?

What part of the original plan had the Spaniards failed to achieve?

Which fleet is more likely to gain the upper hand as time passes? Why?

Fireships

The Spanish had achieved their first objective. The fleet was anchored off Calais having few losses. But here the basic failing of the original plan could be seen. The Duke of Parma wrote to Philip complaining that Medina Sidonia:

> *still wishes me to go out and join him with these boats of ours for us together to attack the enemy's fleet. But it is obviously impossible. The boats are so small there is no room to turn around and the men would fall ill, rot and die.*

The problem was that Medina Sidonia hoped for some small armed vessels known as 'flyboats' to help the larger Spanish vessels to grapple with the English ones. Parma had no flyboats. He only had the small, flat-bottomed boats suitable for ferrying troops across the Channel. These could not be used until, as Parma observed, the wind was fair and the sea clear of enemies!

If the Spanish were dismayed, so too were the English, moored close by. They had hounded the Armada up the Channel, but the gunnery on which they relied had not caused any ship to sink. However, two developments raised their hopes. Firstly the Thames fleet arrived, giving a numerical advantage over the Armada. Secondly Rear Admiral Wynter voiced the thoughts of the other captains when he said:

> *it was not possible to remove them [the Armada] but by a device of firing of ships, which would . . . put many of them in danger of firing and at least make them loose their cables and anchors.*

The decision to use fireships was made. They were not a new idea. Indeed, an Italian expert in fireships named Giambelli was at this time in London working on the defences of the city. Lord Howard had already sent for suitable ships filled with substances that would burn fiercely. However, time was short and instead of waiting Drake volunteered his own ship *Thomas*, and seven others were found. All of them weighed about 150 tons, and their cannons were loaded.

The Spanish also knew of fireships. Medina Sidonia had expected such a trick, and prepared for it by stationing small pinnaces between the fleets, ready to grapple and ward off any fireships. Orders were issued to all ships to make them aware of the danger.

However, the Spaniards were not prepared for the scale of the attack: eight ships all far larger than expected. Even so, there has been some confusion about the effect of the fireships. Here are two different accounts:

A   J. Corbett, a historian who wrote a biography of Drake in 1898.

> *Midnight had passed, the night was at its blackest, and the rushing tide swirled dark and angry through the crowded galleons as they lay*

Parma's army: it has been said that Parma was not keen on the Armada plan. In fairness it was impossible for him to embark his army until the Channel was clear. Had he put to sea in flat barges, the English and the Dutch would have been ready for him

flyboats: flyboats were light, fast warships used for raiding and attacking by the Dutch rebels. Parma had few of these, and could not help Medina Sidonia

Giambelli: Giambelli was an Italian who had designed the 'devil ships of Antwerp'. These were fireships with explosives which had blown up a wooden bridge killing eight hundred men

Fireships. In this reconstruction the artist has combined several events. Having identified the two fleets in the picture, list the differences between this and the written accounts

labouring, each with two anchors out. In the depth of the gloom whence the flood was sweeping with the wind, the English lights were twinkling peacefully, till a sudden flare obscured their brightness. Then another and another burst out, and glowed and grew till eight flaming masses reddened the night, and sped forward with wind and tide upon the terror-stricken Armada. Such a sight man's eyes had never seen. What wonder if a panic seized the Spanish fleet? There was no time to weigh. In reckless haste cables were slipped and cut, and like a herd of stampeding cattle, in mad confusion the tide swept the great fleet away, crashing ship on ship through a tangle of writhing cables.

B The Duke of Medina Sidonia, in his report to Philip of Spain.

At midnight two fires were perceived on the English fleet and these two gradually increased to eight. They were eight vessels with sails set, which were drifting with the current directly towards our flagship and the rest of the Armada, all of them burning with great fury. When the Duke saw them approaching, and that our men had not diverted them, he, fearing that they might contain fire machines or mines, ordered the flagship to let go the cables, the rest of the Armada receiving similar orders, with an intimation that when the fires had passed they were to return to the same positions again. The leading galleass in trying to avoid a ship ran foul of the San Juan de Sicilia, and became so crippled that she was obliged to drift ashore. The current was so strong that although the flagship, and some of the vessels near her, came to anchor again and fired off a signal gun, the other ships of the Armada did not perceive it, and were carried by the current towards Dunkirk.

Exercise

Look carefully at these two documents. Check what each of them has to say about the following points. On which do they agree? On the others, what are the differences?

a) time
b) sea conditions
c) number of fireships
d) Spanish precautions against fireships
e) action taken to avoid fireships
f) mood of the Spanish during the attack
g) damage caused to the fleet by the attack

Is there any reason to believe that one of the accounts might be more reliable than the other? Might both sources have advantages and disadvantages?

Gravelines

In fact not one of the fireships hit its target, but the effect was greater than the English commanders dared hope. They created enough confusion to scatter the Spanish fleet so that the crescent could not possibly be reformed. Medina Sidonia, at his best in this moment of crisis, managed to avoid a fireship and then regain his position. He fired a signal for others to do the same, but when all but three ships failed to respond the *San Martin* followed the fleet to try and regroup them. Soon about thirty ships had rallied to the Duke, and they now prepared for battle.

This was the moment for which the English had been waiting. However, unlike Medina Sidonia, Howard had made a dreadful error of judgement. Soon after the fireships had gone in, one of the galleases, the *San Lorenzo*, had caught a cable and lost its rudder. Howard saw it making slow progress towards the shore and led his

Howard breaking away to attack the galleas

squadron in pursuit. He wanted a rich prize, and had no thought for the rest of the fleet.

Therefore it was Drake who led the main fleet into battle. The action was confused, but witnesses tell of a series of English attacks in which the Spanish ships were heavily bombarded. The difference from the earlier battles in the Channel was that, for the first time the shots were making holes in Spanish hulls.

One Spanish eye-witness described the English attack on the *San Salvador*:

The enemy opened a heavy artillery fire on our flagship, which was to continue for nine hours. So tremendous was the fire that over 200 balls struck the sails and hull of the flagship on the starboard side, killing and wounding many men, disabling and dismounting guns and destroying much rigging. The holes made in the hull between wind and water caused so great a leakage that two divers had as much as they could do to stop them with tow and lead plates working all day.

Steadily a squadron of English ships pounded a victim before moving on to another. To their great credit the Spaniards fought with courage. One dramatic account tells of the *San Felipe*, sails down and upper deck destroyed:

Don Francisco de Toledo ordered the grappling hooks to be brought out and shouted to the enemy to come to close quarters. One Englishman standing in the maintop called out, 'Good soldiers that ye are, surrender to the fair terms we offer ye'. But the only answer he got was a gunshot which brought him down, and the Maestro de Campo then ordered the muskets and harquebuses [heavier muskets] to be brought into action. The English then retired, while our men shouted out to them that they were cowards and Lutheran hens.

Action at Gravelines

The Ark Royal *in combat with a Spanish galleon. From the picture of combat you can get a strong impression of height. What is the object in the top right of the picture? What weapons are in view? What should English tactics be at this moment?*

Other such battles raged as the two fleets continued to sail to the north-west. Howard had now returned to the main battle, which was raging fiercely as the final action was fought. The *San Juan de Sicilia* was one of a number of ships which was badly smashed, and she had 'her portholes all full of blood'. By late afternoon Howard was able to write, 'Their force is wonderful great and strong, but we pluck their feathers little by little'.

The most awful day in the world

Slowly the Spanish fleet was being blown towards the Zeeland sandbanks and the United Provinces of the Netherlands. There the Dutch Protestants were waiting. They hated the Spaniards and regarded them as 'rats to be exterminated'.

However, it was the weather that saved the Armada, first from the English and then from the Dutch. A squall separated the two fleets, giving the Spaniards a chance to dispose of their dead, relieve the wounded and man the pumps. They were numbed and shocked by the battle, and it seemed now that nothing could save them. As one Spaniard said, 'It was the most awful day in the world. Everyone was in utter despair and stood waiting for death'.

Then suddenly, almost miraculously, the wind changed and they found themselves blown by a southerly wind away from the sandbanks and into open sea. Medina Sidonia wrote, 'we were saved by God's mercy'. At least for a little longer the Armada could survive.

The defeat of the Armada

Why had the Armada been so severely mauled at Gravelines when the English fleet had achieved so little before? At Gravelines at least 600 Spaniards died, 800 were wounded, 3 ships were sunk and many more were badly damaged. The English, on the other hand, had lost only fifty men and no ships. Furthermore a survey made within a few weeks of the battle showed no serious damage at all. Consider these documents.

Before Calais a Spaniard reported:

On the 24th, off the Isle of Wight, the enemy attacked our rearguard and showed some signs of a desire to come to closer quarters, but he always avoided coming nearer than artillery range, his plan being to fight only with his ordnance and not to grapple. Although the Duke wished to bring him to close quarters it was impossible because of the swiftness of the enemy's vessels.

At Gravelines, an Englishman reported:

Out of my ship was shot five hundred of demi-cannon, culverin and demi-culverin, and when I was furthest off I was not out of shot of their harquebus and most times within speech of one another.

Exercise
What explains why the Spanish were not damaged in the first clash, but were in the second?

We have already seen that the Spanish had much heavier cannon. Why was it then that when the English shortened their range to 'within jumping distance' the Spanish were unable to make the most of their advantage? The traditional answer is that:

quite early in the fight their stock of roundshot began to give out. Gradually their heavy guns fell silent, and as they did so, the English kept closing the range.

Certainly they were running short, but this would not have happened all at once and their supply was not totally exhausted, as we can see from this report:

Drake's ship was pierced through by several shots of all sizes which were flying everywhere between the two fleets. His cabin was twice pierced by shot and there was one occasion when two gentlemen had retired to rest, one of them lying on the bed, when it was broken to pieces under him by a saker ball. Shortly afterwards it was again hit by ball of a demi-culverin which passed through the cabin from one side to the other taking off the toes of one who was there with them.

Most English shot was from sakers and demi-culverin, and this was causing great damage. Spanish shot from the same size of gun was causing only superficial damage. Why? To solve this problem modern evidence has been needed. Skin divers have brought up shot and cannon from Armada ships:

Analysis shows that the [Spanish] shot was very badly made. The iron itself was full of impurities and it had been quenched while it was still red-hot. Both of these faults would have made it very brittle.

Armada commanders pointed out with pride that all their powder was the fine-grained sort that produced a sharper and harder blow on the shot and the gun. It may well be that most of the Spanish shot broke into small bits either at the shock of firing or the shock of impact on the enemy hull.

The diving revealed that several of the guns that have been retrieved had burst. A gun that burst on a gun deck would have been devastating.

Exercise
Using these documents:

a) What changes were made in English tactics at Gravelines?
b) Is it true that the Spaniards were out of shot?
c) Explain why Spanish shot penetrated Drake's cabin but not the hull of the ship.
d) What was wrong with Spanish shot, and why were they mistaken to use fine-grained powder?
e) Is there any evidence to show that some of the damage suffered by the Spanish at Gravelines was not the result of English fire?

Victors and vanquished

The shattered Armada now headed northwards, followed by the English fleet. Having reached as far as Newcastle most English ships returned southwards. They had run out of ammunition and were short of food, and to make matters worse a storm was rising which forced them into any port they could reach. At first the English captains were unhappy. They did not realise how successful they had been, and they blamed each other for poor tactics. They were also criticised by the Queen, who asked why they had not brought back more prizes. There

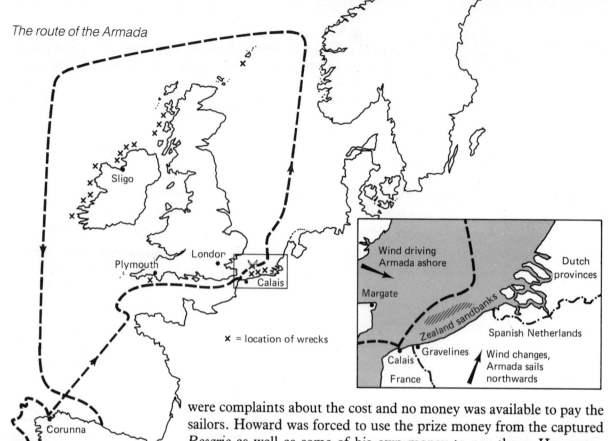

Sligo

London

Plymouth

Calais

✕ = location of wrecks

Corunna

Lisbon

Wind driving
Armada ashore

Margate

Dutch
provinces

Zealand sandbanks

Spanish Netherlands

Calais

Gravelines

France

Wind changes,
Armada sails
northwards

were complaints about the cost and no money was available to pay the sailors. Howard was forced to use the prize money from the captured *Rosario* as well as some of his own money to pay them. He wrote:

> *All I ask is that the crown will put down as much as I have. God knows I am not rich, but I would rather have never a penny in the world than that they should lack.*

It is a sad fact that far more English sailors died of food poisoning and infectious disease while waiting for their pay than were killed by the Spaniards.

But the English fleet was home, whereas the Armada was still heading north, forced on by the wind. A skilled navigator plotted a route home and those ships which stayed with the flagship were all able to follow it. But many other ships were not able to. Some were badly damaged and were forced to seek shelter. Others had only slimy green water and mouldy food, and they had to find fresh supplies to stop their crews from starving. Some went ashore on the coast of England or Scotland.

The worst fate awaited those which were wrecked on the treacherous west coast of Ireland. 1 200 corpses were washed ashore in Sligo Bay alone. Some of the men who escaped the wrecks and swam to the shore were slaughtered as they lay exhausted on the beach. Others were rounded up and taken away to be shot or hanged. Only a very small number were saved from the twenty-five ships which were wrecked on the Irish coast. From the whole Armada the final toll was fifty-one ships and 20 000 men lost.

Ireland: some parts of Ireland were garrisoned by the English. Their hold on Ireland was weak, and they could not risk a Spanish force coming ashore. Other parts were wild, and the Irish there killed the Spaniards to rob them. Only a few were saved for ransom

News of defeat was particularly bitter for Philip of Spain because the earliest reports he had received had been optimistic. There was a rumour that Drake had been captured and a large number of English ships sunk. One source of these rumours was ambassador Mendoza, and Philip wrote to him:

As you consider the news to be true, I am hopeful that it will prove to be so; particularly as the author claims to have been an eye-witness. I am looking for confirmation.

On the same day Philip wrote to Medina Sidonia ending his letter:

I expect that your valour and activity will have accomplished all I could desire.

In fact a letter from Medina Sidonia was already on its way. He explained how the Armada:

was crippled and scattered. Ammunition and the best of our vessels were lacking, and we could little depend upon the ships that remained, the Queen's fleet being so superior to ours in this sort of fighting in consequence of the strength of their artillery and the fast sailing of their ships.

All Philip's hopes were smashed with the Armada. People saw that he received the news with dignity, but that he looked unwell and appeared to have aged years in only a few months. To his credit he did not give up. Alone in his palace he started to work out the plans for a new Armada. As for the old, he wrote to his Bishops:

we are bound to give praise to God for all things which he is pleased to do. In the storms through which the Armada sailed, it might have suffered a worse fate.

Playing cards

The Pope Consulting with his Cardinalls & Contributing a Million of gold towards the Charge of the Armada.

The Prince of Parma coming to Dunkerk with his Army but too late is received by the Spaniards with reproach

More then halfe y Spanish Fleet Taken and Sunck

Our beloved Queen

Elizabeth had played little part in this. Her most important contribution was the speech with which she rallied her subjects:

> *I know I have the body of a weak and feeble woman, but I have the heart and stomach of a king, and of a king of England too; and think foul scorn that Parma or Spain or any prince of Europe should dare invade the borders of my realm: to which, rather than any dishonour shall grow by me, I myself will take up arms.*

The Armada Portrait *is a celebration of the defeat of the Armada. If it is also explaining the reasons for victory, what would it lead us to believe?*

Elizabeth riding through London

But by early September the scale of the victory was clear. The streets of London echoed with rejoicing as banners from the Spanish fleet were displayed at St Paul's and on London Bridge. On 24 November, 1588:

> *The Queen, attended by her Privy council, the Nobility the Judges, the Heralds and Trumpeters all on horseback, came in a chariot drawn by two white horses to St Paul's Church, where, alighting at the west door, she fell on her knees and audibly praised God for her own and the nation's deliverance.*

The war would continue beyond Elizabeth's death, but for now the greatest danger had passed, and her subjects rejoiced in her victory.

Exercise: Why was the Armada defeated

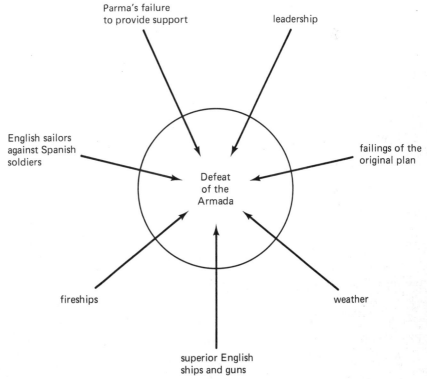

If asked the question 'what caused the defeat of the Spanish Armada?', no single answer would do. The diagram shows a number of *factors* all of which contributed.

a) Can they be arranged in chronological order?
b) Arrange them in order of importance and write a paragraph of supporting evidence about each in answer to the original question. You may also be able to think of some other factors.

INDEX